MASTER THE FACTS

📖 SCHOLAST

MONSTER
MULTIPLICATION
WHEELS

New York • Toronto • London • Auckland • Sydney
Mexico City • New Delhi • Hong Kong • Buenos Aires

Teaching *Resources*

Editor: Mela Ottaiano
Cover and interior design: Jason Robinson
Cover and interior illustrations: Matt Phillips

ISBN-13: 978-0-439-60968-5
ISBN-10: 0-439-60968-2

1 2 3 4 5 6 7 8 9 10   40   14 13 12 11 10 09 08

CONTENTS

INTRODUCTION

Welcome to *Monster Multiplication Wheels*, an engaging collection of hands-on learning manipulatives. The easy-to-make, fun-to-use wheels teach and reinforce the multiplication facts between 1 and 12. Because the wheels are self-correcting, students can practice independently until they master these essential math facts.

In this book you'll find a reproducible multiplication table (page 6), one wheel for each set of facts, ten wheels containing mixed facts, and a blank template that you (or students) can customize. There are also assessments and quizzes (pages 53–60) to help track students' progress followed by reproducible reward certificates.

TIP Help students understand that zero is a very special number in multiplication. A number multiplied by 0 is always equal to 0. Consider including some zero multiplication facts when you create your own wheels.

Using the Pre- and Post-Assessment Quizzes

Prior to handing out the first wheel pattern, give students a pre-assessment quiz. Each multiplication fact family is represented on the pre- and post-assessment quizzes, so you will be able to get a general sense of the fact families students may need to focus on, either individually or as a class. When you determine it is appropriate, administer the post-assessment quiz to see how students' mastery has developed.

Using the Self-Checking Quizzes

After students have spent time using the monster multiplication wheel for a particular multiplication fact family, have them take a self-checking quiz. First, photocopy the page containing the appropriate fact family and cut it in half along the dotted line. Save the remaining quiz to hand out as needed. Next, fold over the gray panel so the answers are covered. Then, distribute the sheets to students and have them fill in their answers. Finally, they may lift the panel to reveal the correct answers and check their own work. If you determine it's necessary, ask students to engage in additional practice using the wheel. Working with "the monsters" will help students have fun and stay motivated to stick with the practice.

Making the Monster Multiplication Wheels

Each multiplication facts wheel is created from two pages: one with a master-the-facts monster and one with numbers. Although you and/or parent volunteers can easily construct the wheels, it's a good opportunity for students to exercise their direction-following skills if you involve them in creating the wheels. First, photocopy the How to Make a Monster Multiplication Wheel directions on the next page and set of patterns for each student. (Copy the wheel patterns onto card stock, if possible.) Students will also need crayons or markers for coloring in the monsters, scissors for cutting out the patterns, and brass fasteners for securing the top and bottom pages.

How to Make a Monster Multiplication Wheel

MATERIALS

- wheel patterns (2 pages)
- crayons or markers
- scissors
- brass fastener

DIRECTIONS

1. Color in your master-the-facts monster.
2. Cut out each wheel along the solid line.
3. Cut out the fact opening and answer flap along the dotted lines.
4. Place the monster wheel on top of the numbers wheel.
5. Line up the crosses in the center. Push a brass fastener through the crosses and open at the back. (See the diagram below.)

Now you're ready to turn to learn!

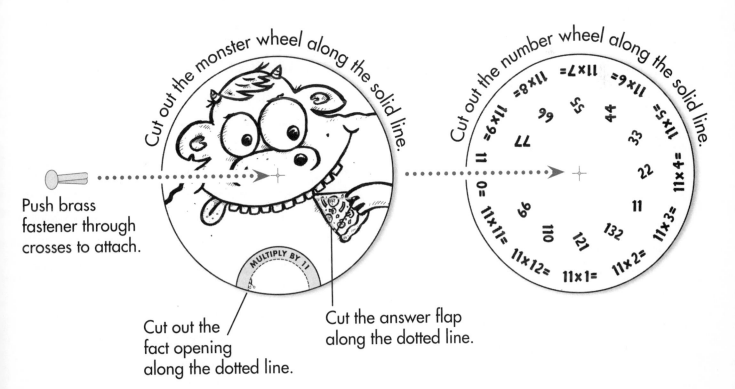

Push brass fastener through crosses to attach.

Cut out the fact opening along the dotted line.

Cut the answer flap along the dotted line.

Multiplication Table

x	0	1	2	3	4	5	6	7	8	9	10	11	12
0	0	0	0	0	0	0	0	0	0	0	0	0	0
1	0	1	2	3	4	5	6	7	8	9	10	11	12
2	0	2	4	6	8	10	12	14	16	18	20	22	24
3	0	3	6	9	12	15	18	21	24	27	30	33	36
4	0	4	8	12	16	20	24	28	32	36	40	44	48
5	0	5	10	15	20	25	30	35	40	45	50	55	60
6	0	6	12	18	24	30	36	42	48	54	60	66	72
7	0	7	14	21	28	35	42	49	56	63	70	77	84
8	0	8	16	24	32	40	48	56	64	72	80	88	96
9	0	9	18	27	36	45	54	63	72	81	90	99	108
10	0	10	20	30	40	50	60	70	80	90	100	110	120
11	0	11	22	33	44	55	66	77	88	99	110	121	132
12	0	12	24	36	48	60	72	84	96	108	120	132	144

Multiplying by 1

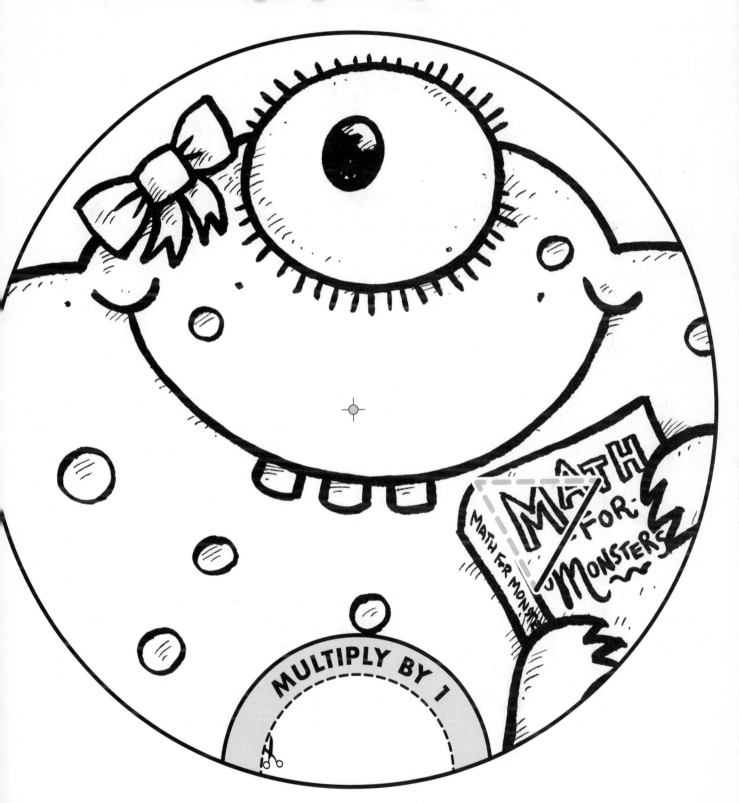

Multiplying by 1

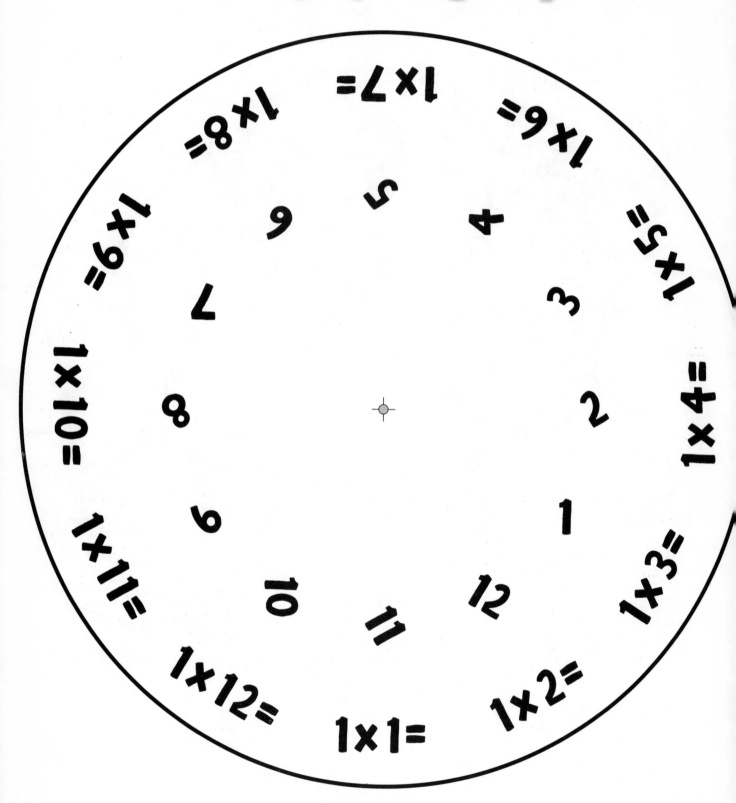

Monster Multiplication Wheels © 2008 Scholastic I

Multiplying by 2

MULTIPLY BY 2

Multiplying by 2

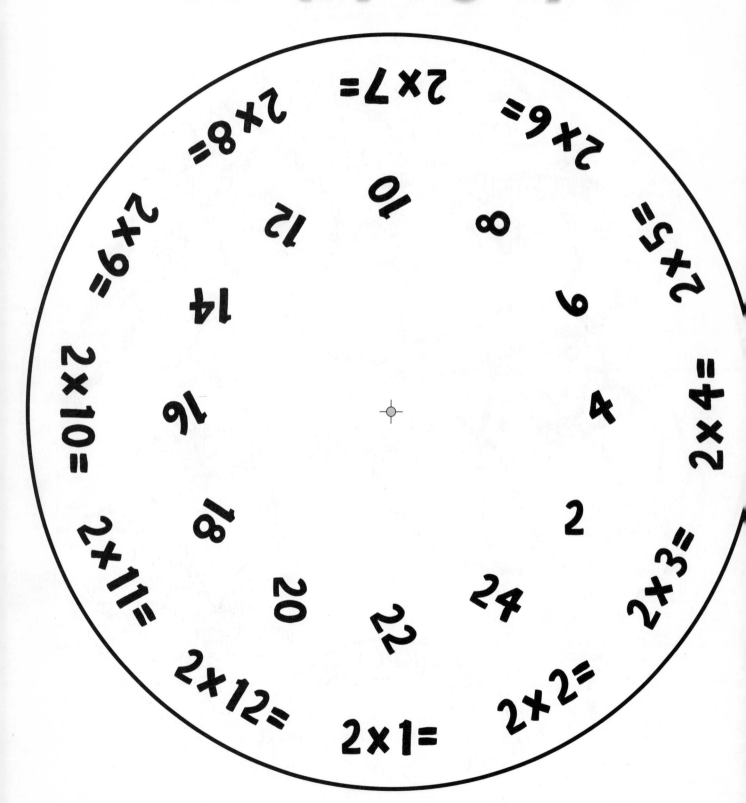

Multiplying by 3

MULTIPLY BY 3

Multiplying by 3

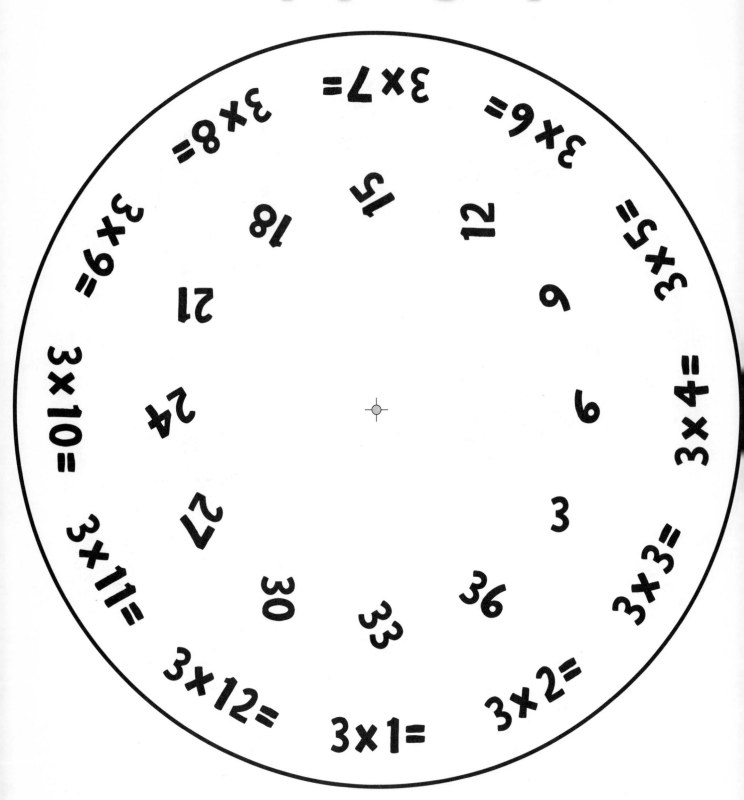

Multiplying by 4

MULTIPLY BY 4

Multiplying by 4

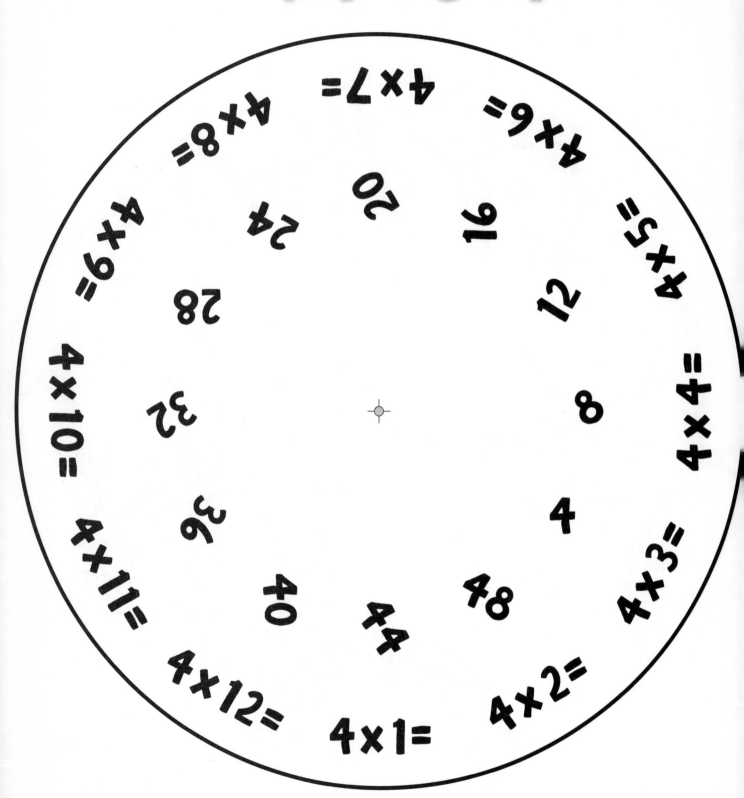

Multiplying by 5

MULTIPLY BY 5

Multiplying by 5

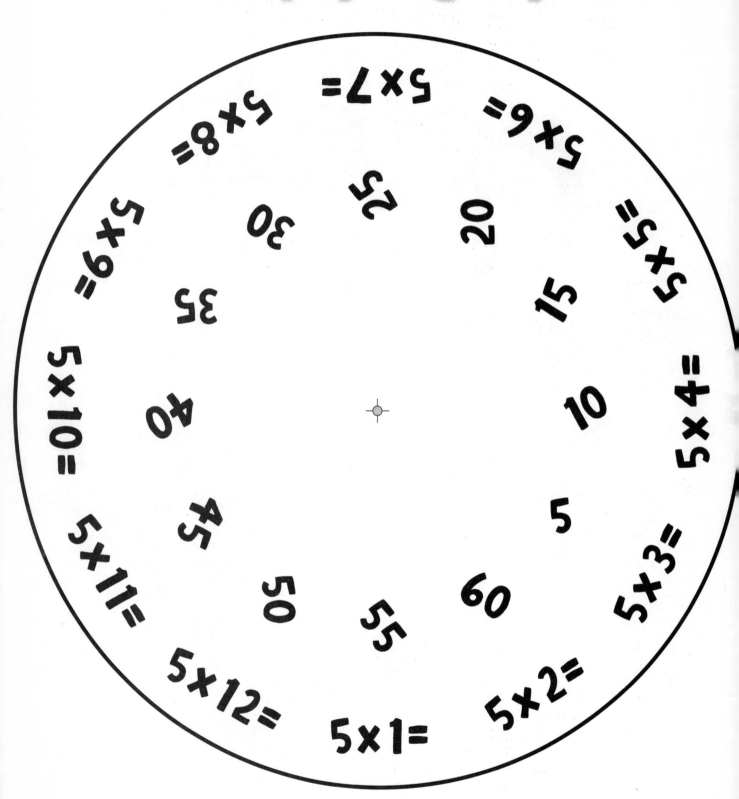

Multiplying by 6

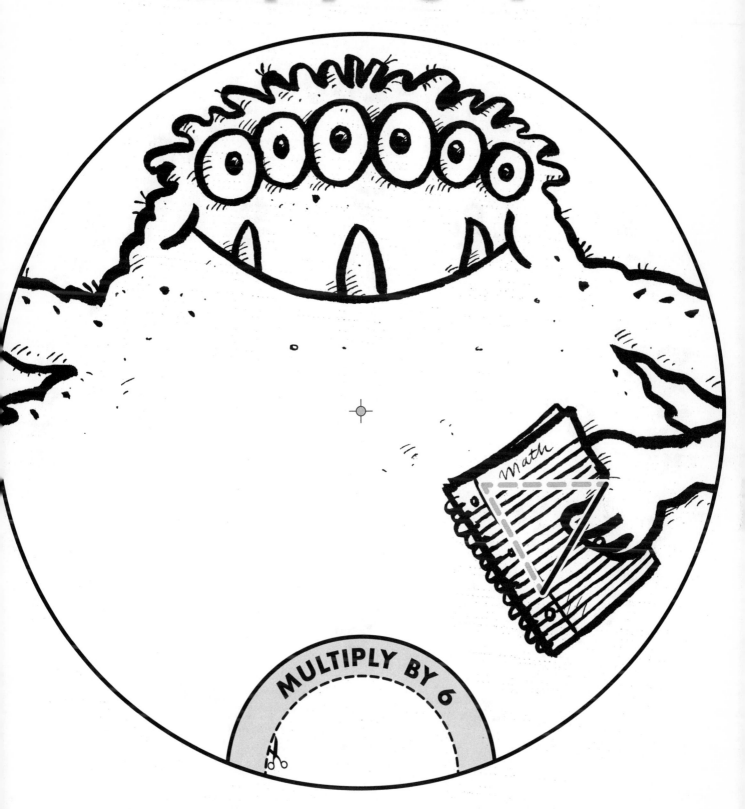

MULTIPLY BY 6

Multiplying by 6

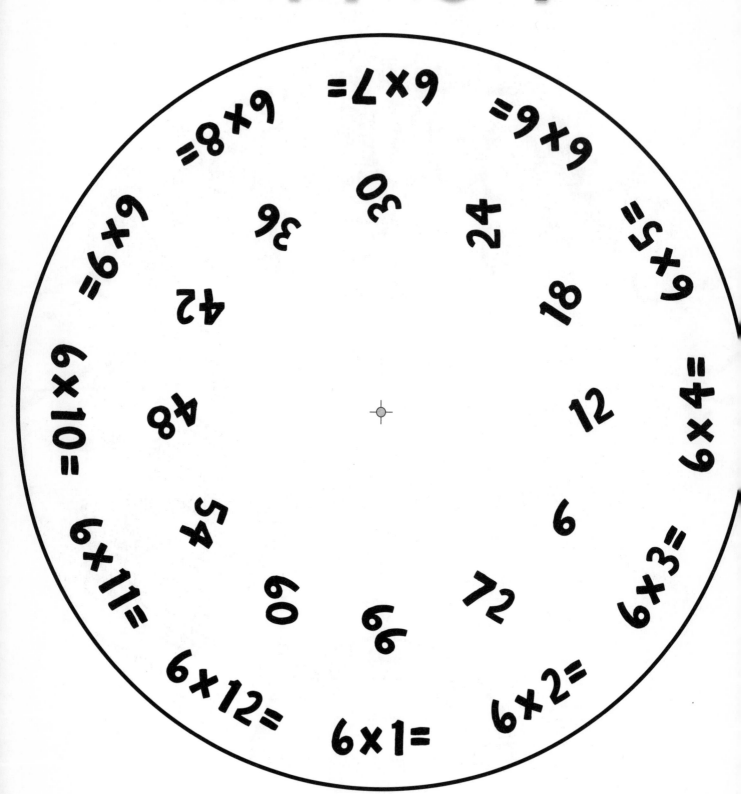

Multiplying by 7

MULTIPLY BY 7

Multiplying by 7

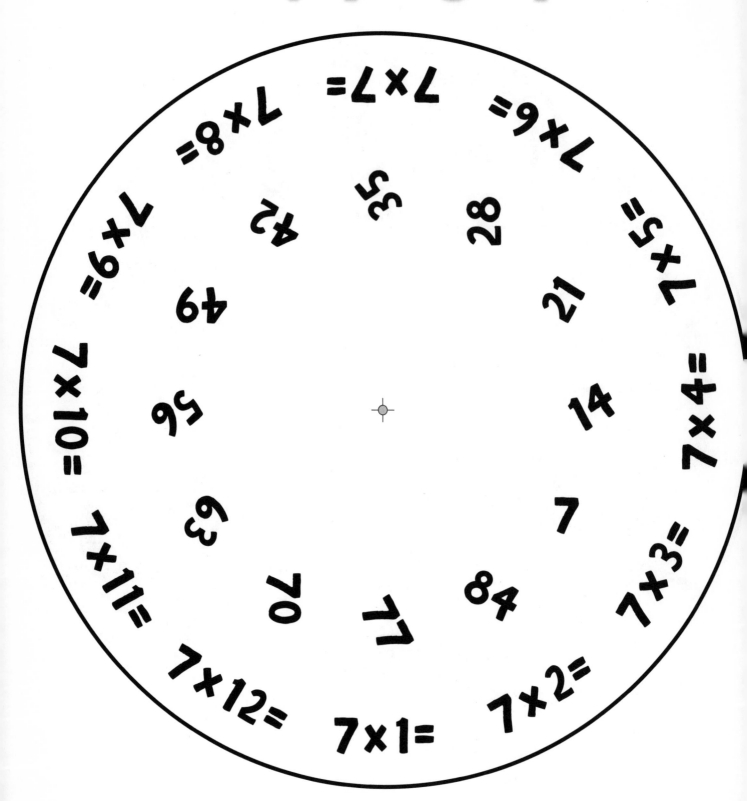

Multiplying by 8

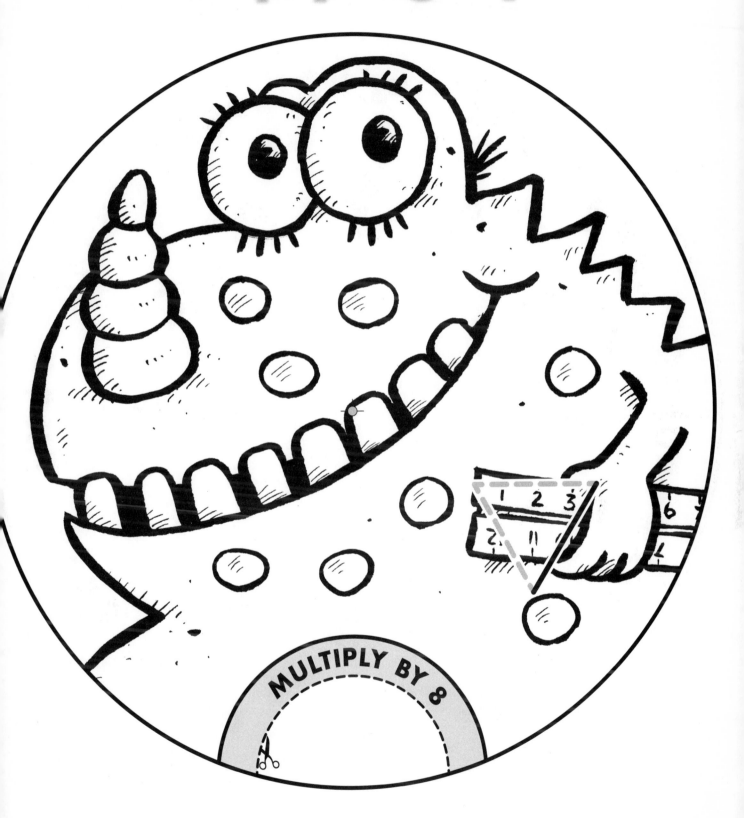

MULTIPLY BY 8

Multiplying by 8

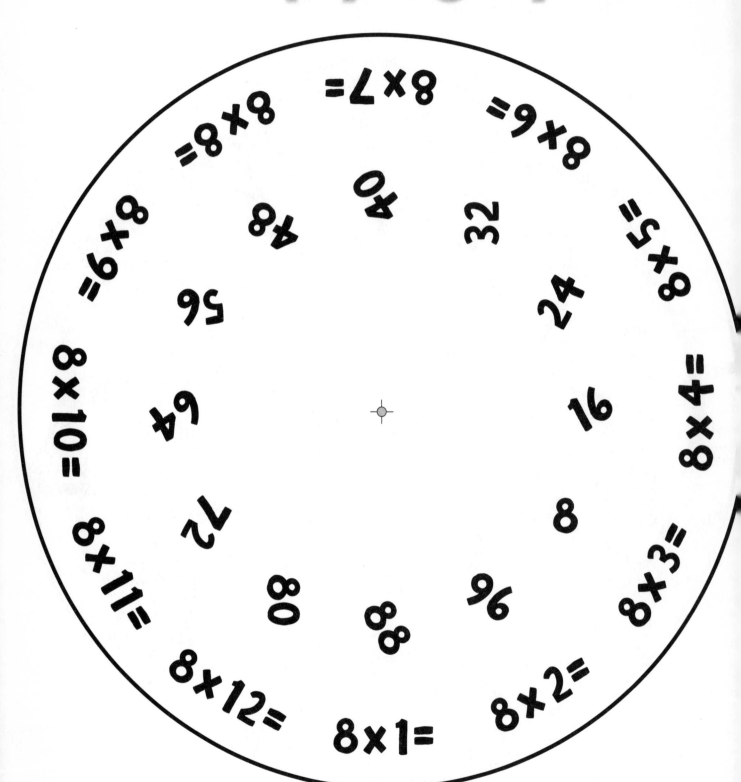

Multiplying by 9

MULTIPLY BY 9

23

Multiplying by 9

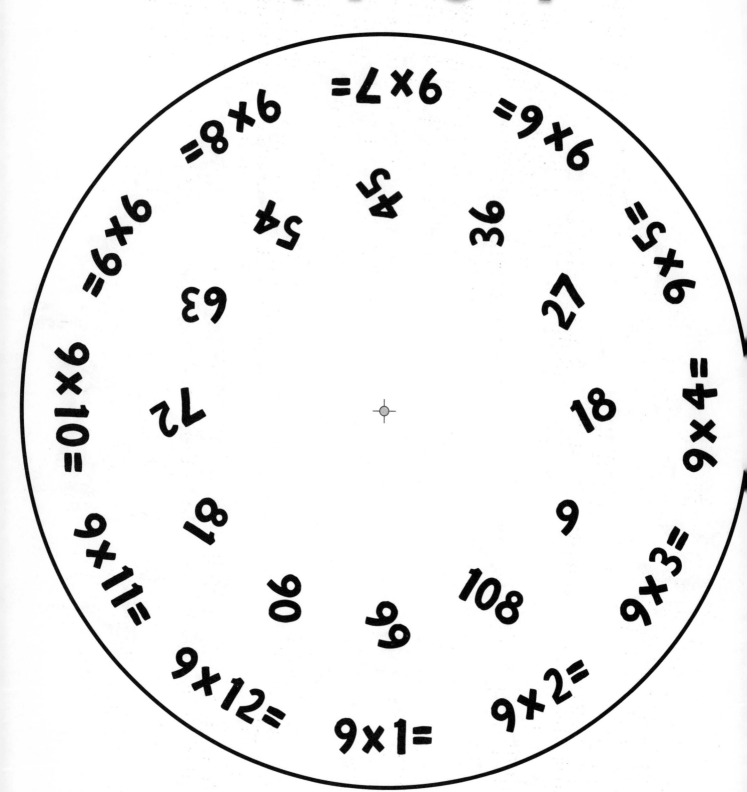

Multiplying by 10

MULTIPLY BY 10

Multiplying by 10

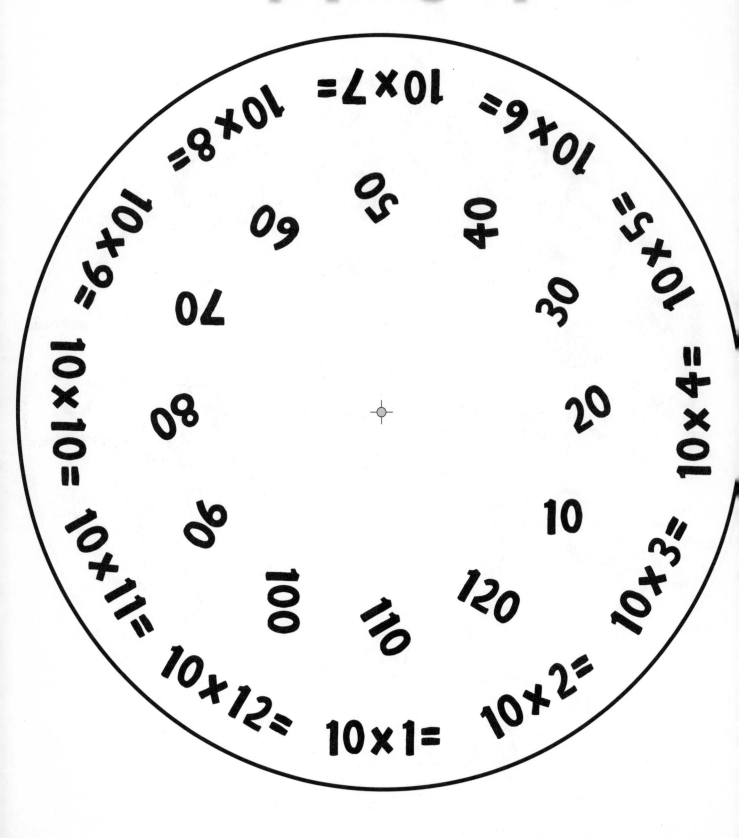

Multiplying by 11

MULTIPLY BY 11

Multiplying by 11

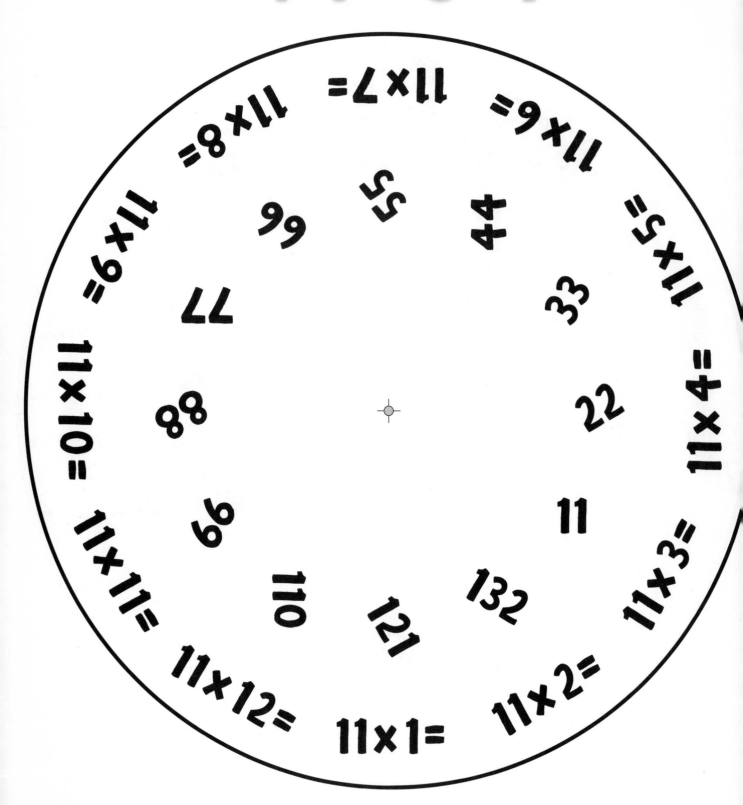

Multiplying by 12

MULTIPLY BY 12

Multiplying by 12

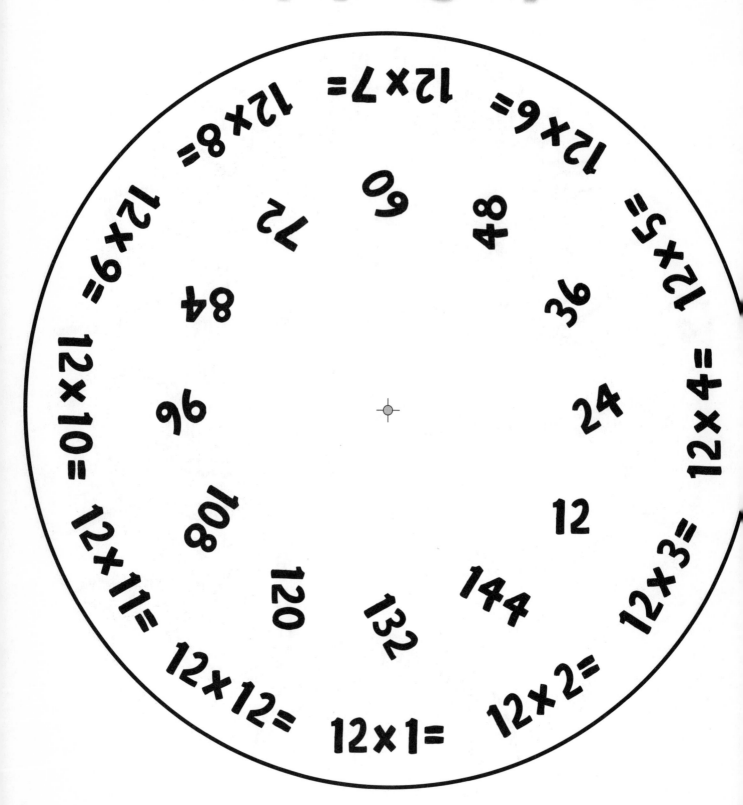

Multiplying by 1 and 2

MULTIPLY BY 1 AND 2

Multiplying by 1 and 2

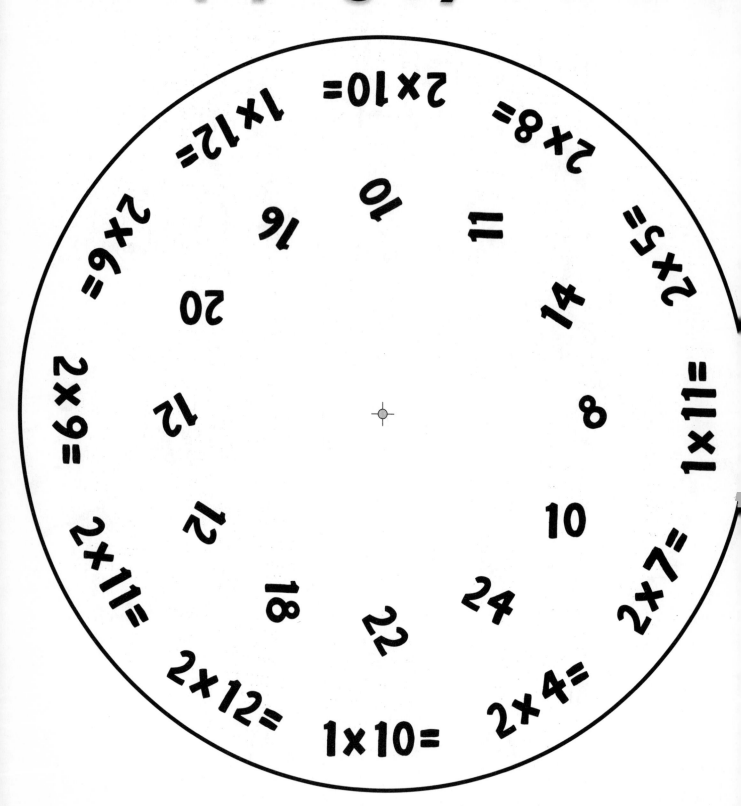

Multiplying by 3 and 4

MULTIPLY BY 3 AND 4

Multiplying by 3 and 4

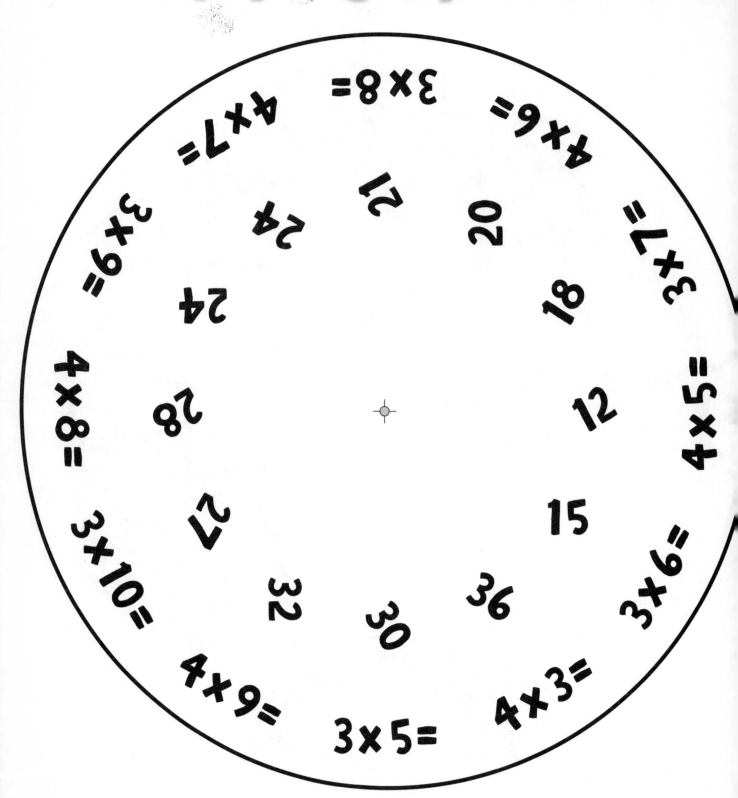

Multiplying by 5 and 6

MULTIPLY BY 5 AND 6

Multiplying by 5 and 6

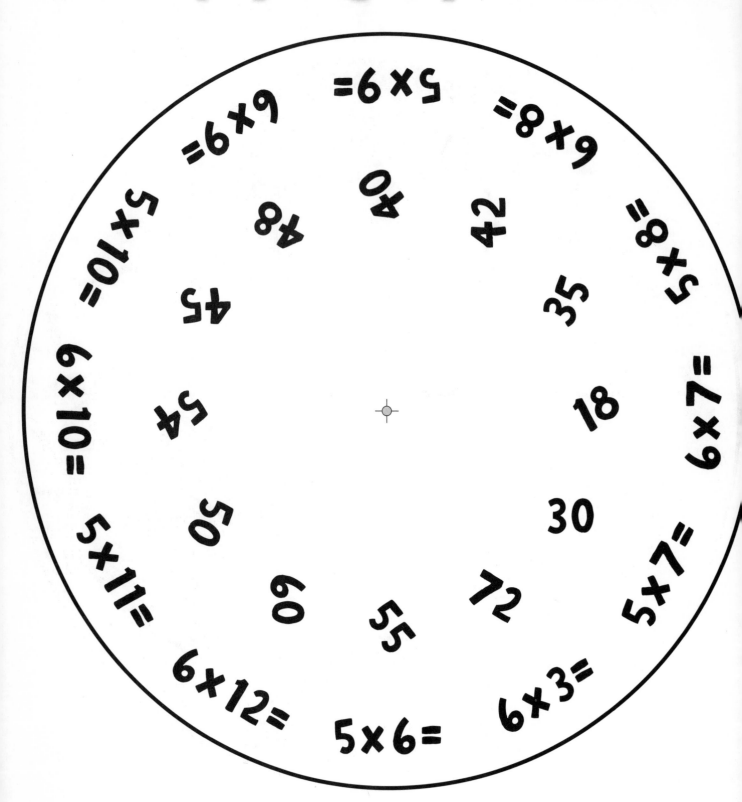

Multiplying by 7 and 8

Multiplying by 7 and 8

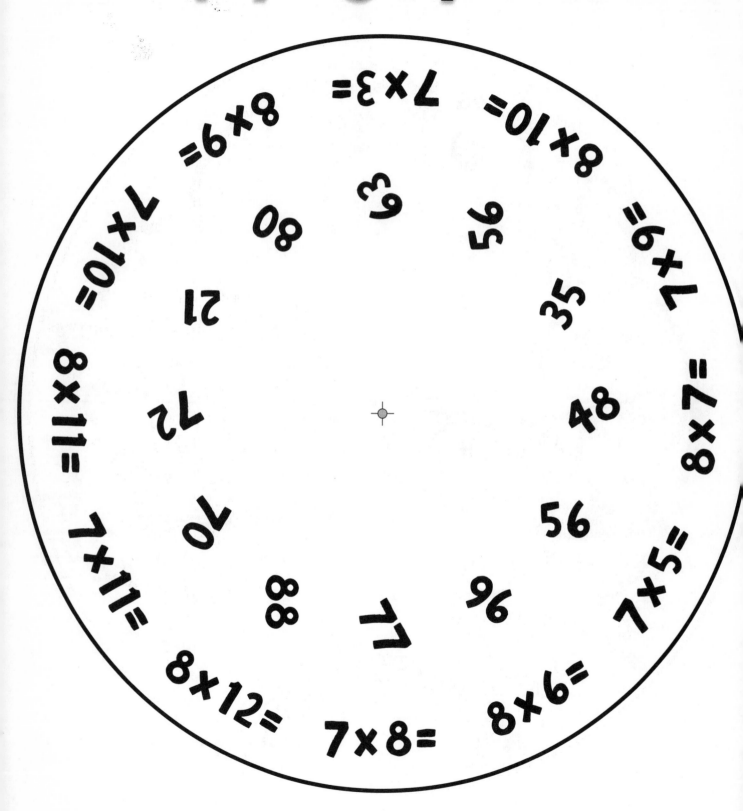

MULTIPLY BY 9 AND 10

Multiplying by 9 and 10

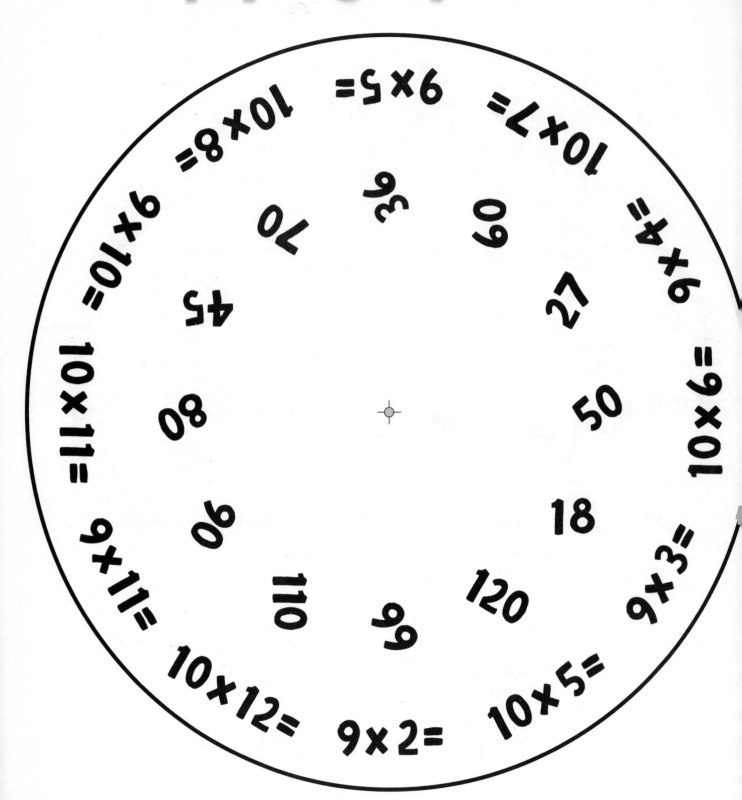

Multiplying by 11 and 12

Multiplying by 11 and 12

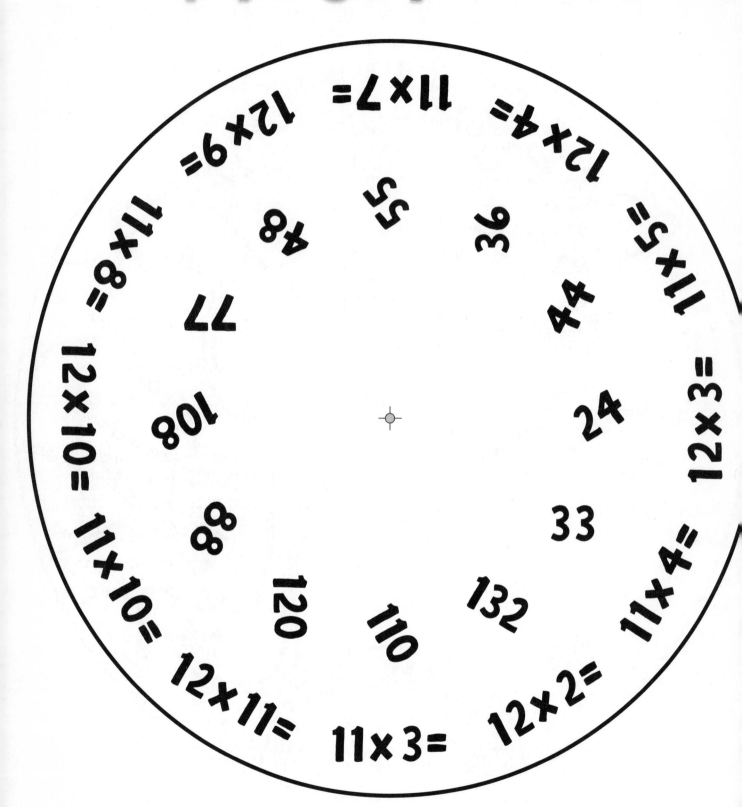

Multiplying Doubles

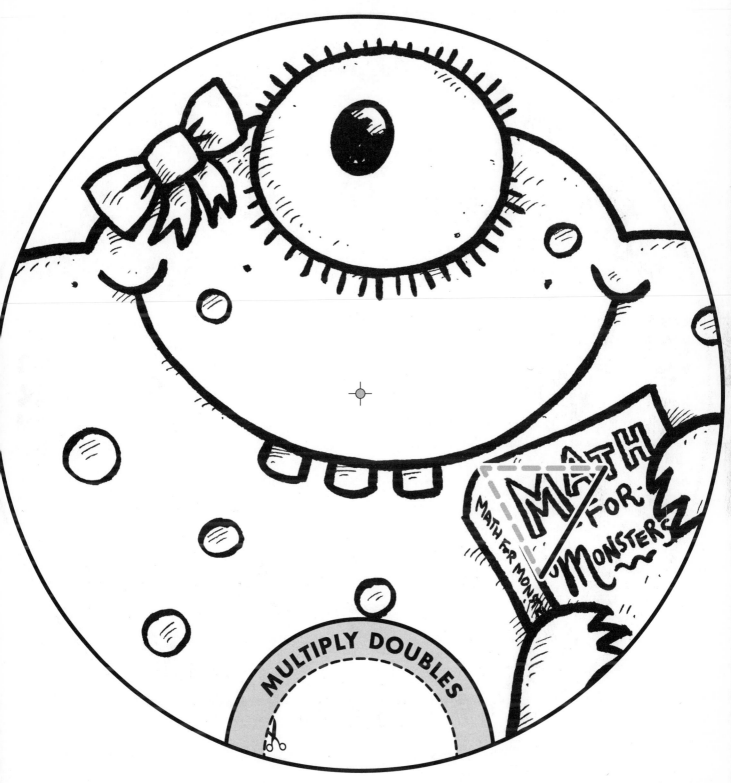

MULTIPLY DOUBLES

MATH FOR MONSTERS

Multiplying Doubles

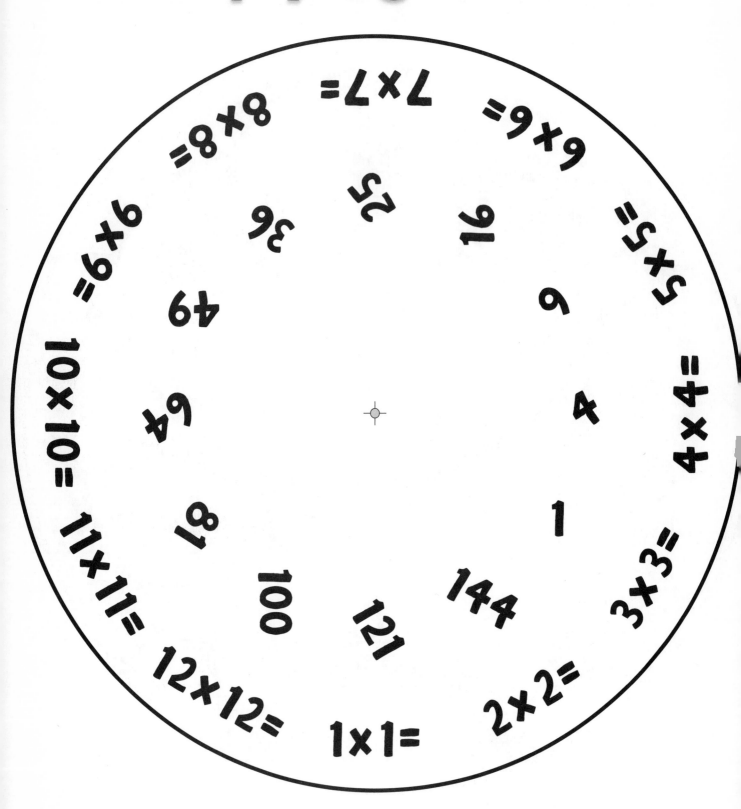

Multiplying by 4, 5, and 6

MULTIPLY BY 4, 5, AND 6

Multiplying by 4, 5, and 6

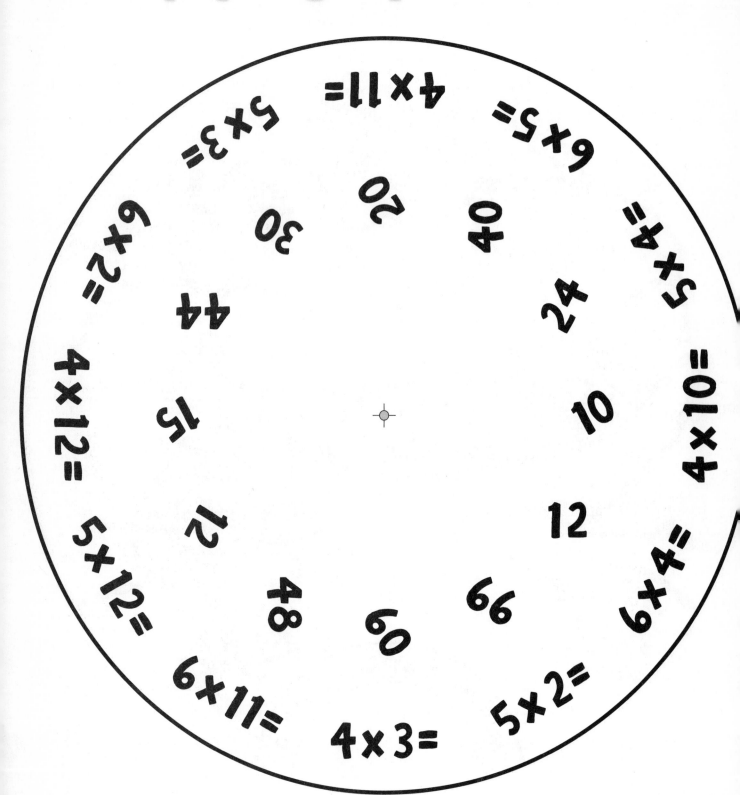

Monster Multiplication Wheels © 2008 Scholastic

MULTIPLY BY 7, 8, AND 9

Multiplying by 7, 8, and 9

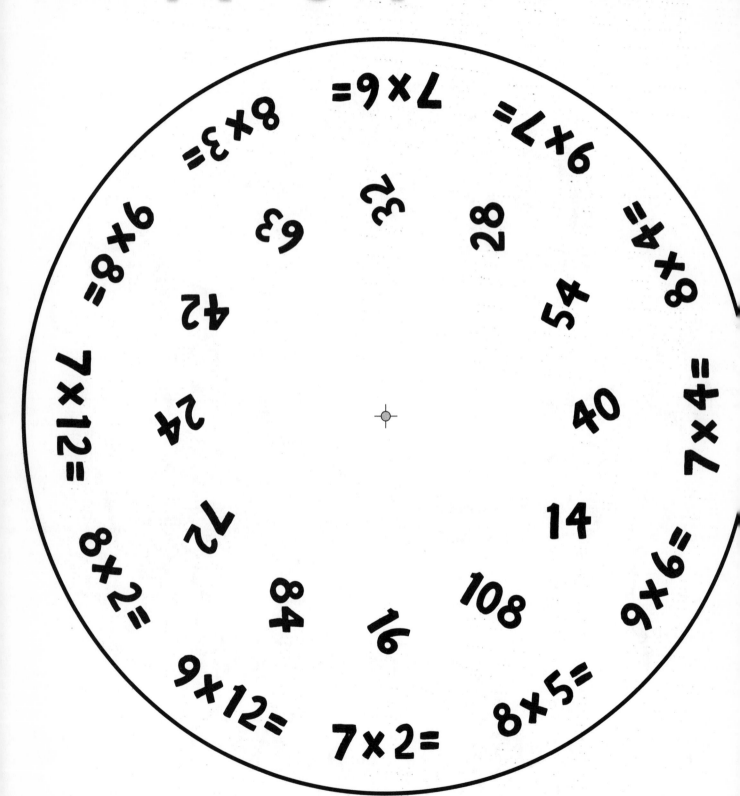

Monster Multiplication Wheels © 2008 Scholastic

Multiplying by 10, 11, and 12

MULTIPLY BY 10, 11, AND 12

Multiplying by 10, 11, and 12

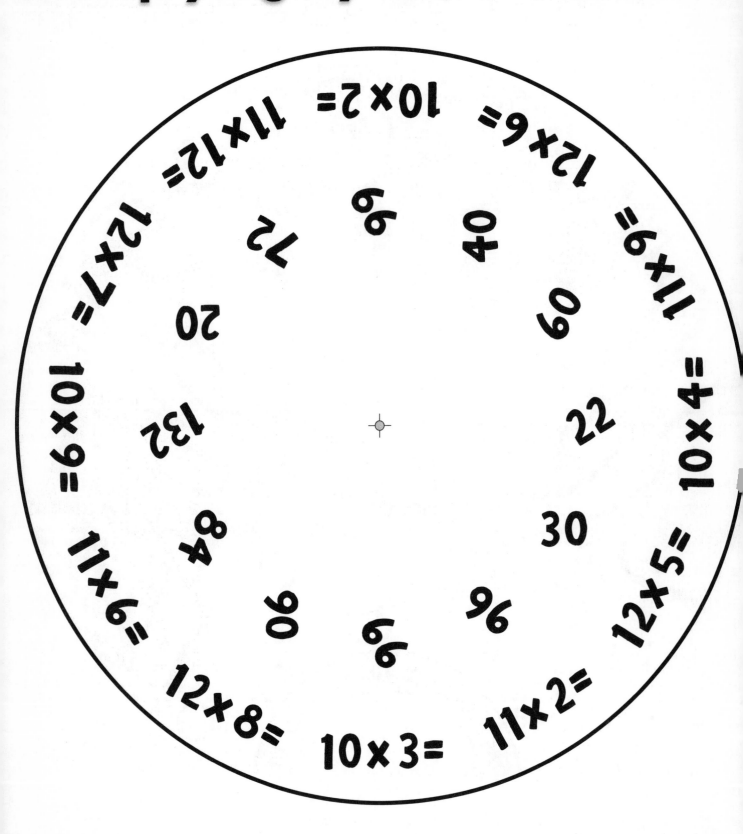

Multiplying by ________

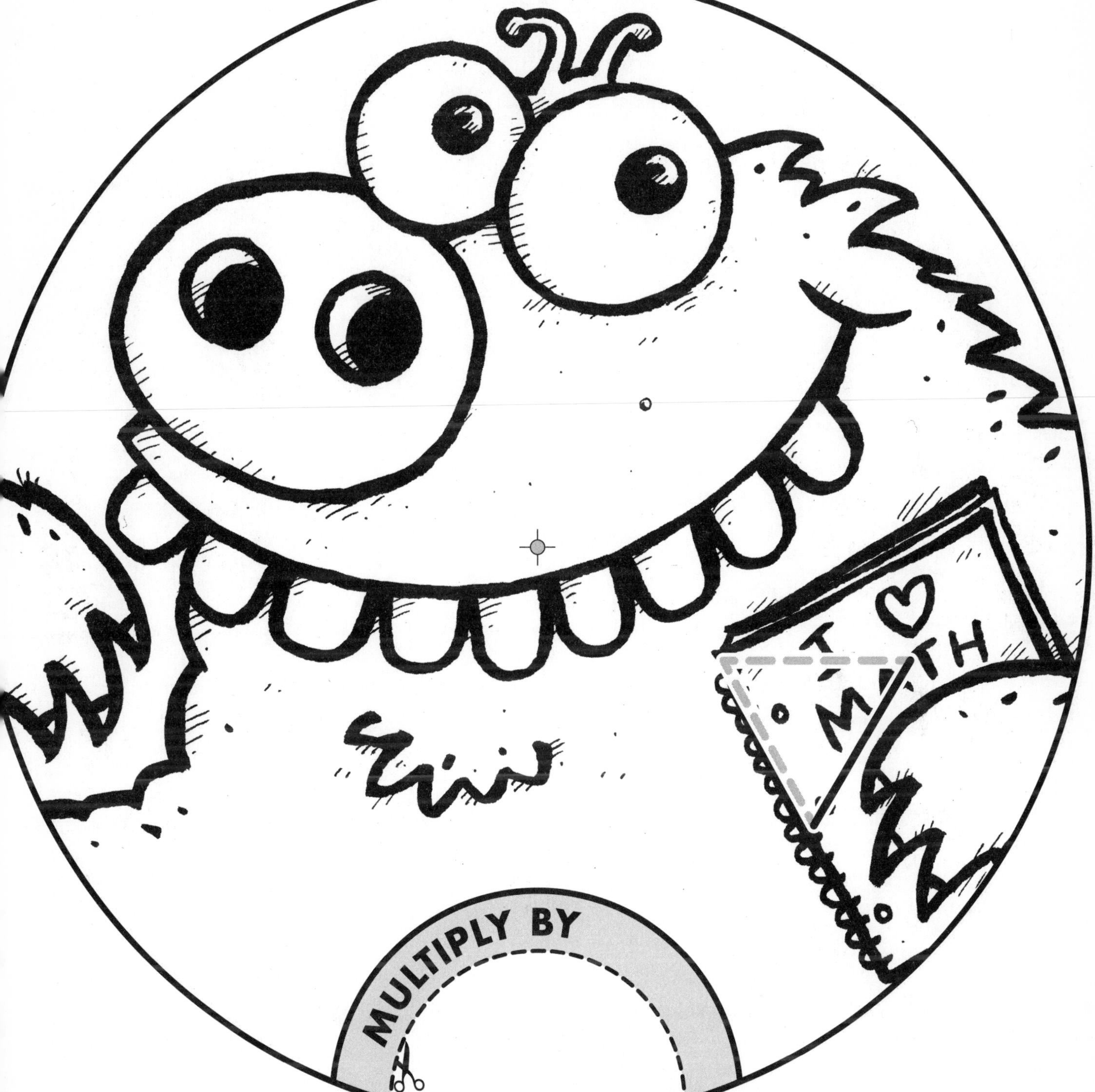

Multiplying by _____

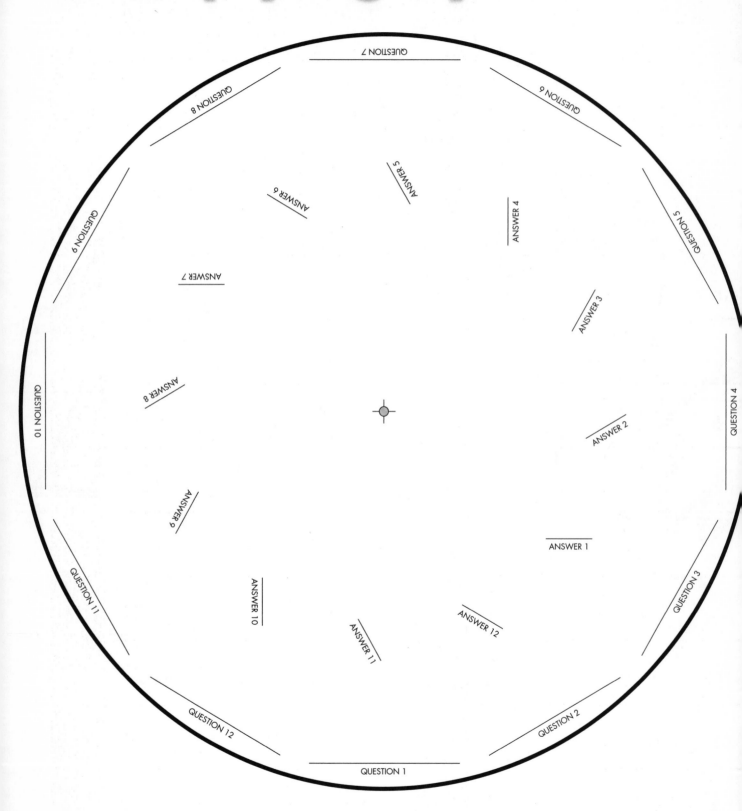

QUESTION 7

QUESTION 8

QUESTION 6

QUESTION 9

ANSWER 5

ANSWER 6

ANSWER 4

QUESTION 5

ANSWER 7

ANSWER 3

QUESTION 10

ANSWER 8

ANSWER 2

QUESTION 4

ANSWER 1

ANSWER 9

QUESTION 11

QUESTION 3

ANSWER 10

ANSWER 12

ANSWER 11

QUESTION 12

QUESTION 2

QUESTION 1

Self-Checking Quiz: Multiplying by 1

1.	$1 \times 1 =$ _____	1
2.	$1 \times 2 =$ _____	2
3.	$1 \times 3 =$ _____	3
4.	$1 \times 4 =$ _____	4
5.	$1 \times 5 =$ _____	5
6.	$1 \times 6 =$ _____	6
7.	$1 \times 7 =$ _____	7
8.	$1 \times 8 =$ _____	8
9.	$1 \times 9 =$ _____	9
10.	$1 \times 10 =$ _____	10
11.	$1 \times 11 =$ _____	11
12.	$12 \times 12 =$ _____	12

Self-Checking Quiz: Multiplying by 2

1.	$2 \times 1 =$ _____	2
2.	$2 \times 2 =$ _____	4
3.	$2 \times 3 =$ _____	6
4.	$2 \times 4 =$ _____	8
5.	$2 \times 5 =$ _____	10
6.	$2 \times 6 =$ _____	12
7.	$2 \times 7 =$ _____	14
8.	$2 \times 8 =$ _____	16
9.	$2 \times 9 =$ _____	18
10.	$2 \times 10 =$ _____	20
11.	$2 \times 11 =$ _____	22
12.	$2 \times 12 =$ _____	24

Name _____ Date _____

Name _____ Date _____

Self-Checking Quiz: Multiplying by 3

1.	$3 \times 1 =$ _____	3
2.	$3 \times 2 =$ _____	6
3.	$3 \times 3 =$ _____	9
4.	$3 \times 4 =$ _____	12
5.	$3 \times 5 =$ _____	15
6.	$3 \times 6 =$ _____	18
7.	$3 \times 7 =$ _____	21
8.	$3 \times 8 =$ _____	24
9.	$3 \times 9 =$ _____	27
10.	$3 \times 10 =$ _____	30
11.	$3 \times 11 =$ _____	33
12.	$3 \times 12 =$ _____	36

Self-Checking Quiz: Multiplying by 4

1.	$4 \times 1 =$ _____	4
2.	$4 \times 2 =$ _____	8
3.	$4 \times 3 =$ _____	12
4.	$4 \times 4 =$ _____	16
5.	$4 \times 5 =$ _____	20
6.	$4 \times 6 =$ _____	24
7.	$4 \times 7 =$ _____	28
8.	$4 \times 8 =$ _____	32
9.	$4 \times 9 =$ _____	36
10.	$4 \times 10 =$ _____	40
11.	$4 \times 11 =$ _____	44
12.	$4 \times 12 =$ _____	48

Self-Checking Quiz: Multiplying by 5

1.	$5 \times 1 =$ _____	5
2.	$5 \times 2 =$ _____	10
3.	$5 \times 3 =$ _____	15
4.	$5 \times 4 =$ _____	20
5.	$5 \times 5 =$ _____	25
6.	$5 \times 6 =$ _____	30
7.	$5 \times 7 =$ _____	35
8.	$5 \times 8 =$ _____	40
9.	$5 \times 9 =$ _____	45
10.	$5 \times 10 =$ _____	50
11.	$5 \times 11 =$ _____	55
12.	$5 \times 12 =$ _____	60

Self-Checking Quiz: Multiplying by 6

1.	$6 \times 1 =$ _____	6
2.	$6 \times 2 =$ _____	12
3.	$6 \times 3 =$ _____	18
4.	$6 \times 4 =$ _____	24
5.	$6 \times 5 =$ _____	30
6.	$6 \times 6 =$ _____	36
7.	$6 \times 7 =$ _____	42
8.	$6 \times 8 =$ _____	48
9.	$6 \times 9 =$ _____	54
10.	$6 \times 10 =$ _____	60
11.	$6 \times 11 =$ _____	66
12.	$6 \times 12 =$ _____	72

Self-Checking Quiz: Multiplying by 7

1.	7 x 1 = _____	7
2.	7 x 2 = _____	14
3.	7 x 3 = _____	21
4.	7 x 4 = _____	28
5.	7 x 5 = _____	35
6.	7 x 6 = _____	42
7.	7 x 7 = _____	49
8.	7 x 8 = _____	56
9.	7 x 9 = _____	63
10.	7 x 10 = _____	70
11.	7 x 11 = _____	77
12.	7 x 12 = _____	84

Self-Checking Quiz: Multiplying by 8

1.	8 x 1 = _____	8
2.	8 x 2 = _____	16
3.	8 x 3 = _____	24
4.	8 x 4 = _____	32
5.	8 x 5 = _____	40
6.	8 x 6 = _____	48
7.	8 x 7 = _____	56
8.	8 x 8 = _____	64
9.	8 x 9 = _____	72
10.	8 x 10 = _____	80
11.	8 x 11 = _____	88
12.	8 x 12 = _____	96

Self-Checking Quiz: Multiplying by 9	**Self-Checking Quiz: Multiplying by 10**

#	Problem	Answer	#	Problem	Answer
1.	$9 \times 1 =$ ____	9	1.	$10 \times 1 =$ ____	10
2.	$9 \times 2 =$ ____	18	2.	$10 \times 2 =$ ____	20
3.	$9 \times 3 =$ ____	27	3.	$10 \times 3 =$ ____	30
4.	$9 \times 4 =$ ____	36	4.	$10 \times 4 =$ ____	40
5.	$9 \times 5 =$ ____	45	5.	$10 \times 5 =$ ____	50
6.	$9 \times 6 =$ ____	54	6.	$10 \times 6 =$ ____	60
7.	$9 \times 7 =$ ____	63	7.	$10 \times 7 =$ ____	70
8.	$9 \times 8 =$ ____	72	8.	$10 \times 8 =$ ____	80
9.	$9 \times 9 =$ ____	81	9.	$10 \times 9 =$ ____	90
10.	$9 \times 10 =$ ____	90	10.	$10 \times 10 =$ ____	100
11.	$9 \times 11 =$ ____	99	11.	$10 \times 11 =$ ____	110
12.	$9 \times 12 =$ ____	108	12.	$10 \times 12 =$ ____	120

Name _____ Date _____

Self-Checking Quiz: Multiplying by 11

1. $11 \times 1 =$ _____ 11

2. $11 \times 2 =$ _____ 22

3. $11 \times 3 =$ _____ 33

4. $11 \times 4 =$ _____ 44

5. $11 \times 5 =$ _____ 55

6. $11 \times 6 =$ _____ 66

7. $11 \times 7 =$ _____ 77

8. $11 \times 8 =$ _____ 88

9. $11 \times 9 =$ _____ 99

10. $11 \times 10 =$ _____ 110

11. $11 \times 11 =$ _____ 121

12. $11 \times 12 =$ _____ 132

Name _____ Date _____

Self-Checking Quiz: Multiplying by 12

1. $12 \times 1 =$ _____ 12

2. $12 \times 2 =$ _____ 24

3. $12 \times 3 =$ _____ 36

4. $12 \times 4 =$ _____ 48

5. $12 \times 5 =$ _____ 60

6. $12 \times 6 =$ _____ 72

7. $12 \times 7 =$ _____ 84

8. $12 \times 8 =$ _____ 96

9. $12 \times 9 =$ _____ 108

10. $12 \times 10 =$ _____ 120

11. $12 \times 11 =$ _____ 132

12. $12 \times 12 =$ _____ 144

Pre-Assessment

1.	2 x 2 = _____		**16.**	10 x 8 = _____
2.	3 x 4 = _____		**17.**	12 x 10 = _____
3.	1 x 6 = _____		**18.**	3 x 12 = _____
4.	5 x 8 = _____		**19.**	5 x 3 = _____
5.	6 x 10 = _____		**20.**	7 x 5 = _____
6.	7 x 12 = _____		**21.**	9 x 7 = _____
7.	8 x 1 = _____		**22.**	11 x 1 = _____
8.	9 x 3 = _____		**23.**	5 x 12 = _____
9.	10 x 5 = _____		**24.**	6 x 2 = _____
10.	11 x 7 = _____		**25.**	7 x 3 = _____
11.	12 x 9 = _____		**26.**	8 x 4 = _____
12.	2 x 11 = _____		**27.**	9 x 8 = _____
13.	4 x 2 = _____		**28.**	10 x 9 = _____
14.	6 x 4 = _____		**29.**	11 x 10 = _____
15.	8 x 6 = _____		**30.**	12 x 12 = _____

Name _____ Date _____ Score $\boxed{30}$

Post-Assessment

1. 4 x 4 = _____

2. 3 x 11 = _____

3. 2 x 3 = _____

4. 5 x 6 = _____

5. 7 x 7 = _____

6. 12 x 6 = _____

7. 8 x 7 = _____

8. 9 x 5 = _____

9. 10 x 3 = _____

10. 11 x 9 = _____

11. 12 x 7 = _____

12. 2 x 10 = _____

13. 4 x 5 = _____

14. 6 x 3 = _____

15. 8 x 2 = _____

16. 10 x 1 = _____

17. 12 x 11 = _____

18. 3 x 8 = _____

19. 5 x 2 = _____

20. 5 x 7 = _____

21. 9 x 9 = _____

22. 11 x 4 = _____

23. 8 x 8 = _____

24. 6 x 12 = _____

25. 7 x 9 = _____

26. 8 x 5 = _____

27. 8 x 9 = _____

28. 4 x 12 = _____

29. 7 x 10 = _____

30. 11 x 11 = _____

60

CONGRATULATIONS!

Great!

_____
NAME

HAS MASTERED THE
1 **TIMES TABLE!**

_____   _____
TEACHER   DATE

CONGRATULATIONS!

Wow!

_____
NAME

HAS MASTERED THE
2 **TIMES TABLE!**

_____   _____
TEACHER   DATE

CONGRATULATIONS!

Super!

_____
NAME

HAS MASTERED THE
3 **TIMES TABLE!**

_____   _____
TEACHER   DATE

CONGRATULATIONS!

Great

_____
NAME

HAS MASTERED THE
4 TIMES TABLE!

_____ _____
TEACHER   DATE

CONGRATULATIONS!

Wow!

_____
NAME

HAS MASTERED THE
5 TIMES TABLE!

_____ _____
TEACHER   DATE

CONGRATULATIONS!

Super

_____
NAME

HAS MASTERED THE
6 TIMES TABLE!

_____ _____
TEACHER   DATE

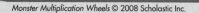

CONGRATULATIONS!

Great!

_____
NAME

HAS MASTERED THE 7 TIMES TABLE!

_____   _____
TEACHER   DATE

CONGRATULATIONS!

Wow!

_____
NAME

HAS MASTERED THE 8 TIMES TABLE!

_____   _____
TEACHER   DATE

CONGRATULATIONS!

Super!

_____
NAME

HAS MASTERED THE 9 TIMES TABLE!

_____   _____
TEACHER   DATE

CONGRATULATIONS!

Great

_____
NAME

HAS MASTERED THE
10 TIMES TABLE!

_____   _____
TEACHER   DATE

CONGRATULATIONS!

Wow!

_____
NAME

HAS MASTERED THE
11 TIMES TABLE!

_____   _____
TEACHER   DATE

CONGRATULATIONS!

Super

_____
NAME

HAS MASTERED THE
12 TIMES TABLE!

_____   _____
TEACHER   DATE